# AND

# PARDON

## The

# Parable

## of the

# Prodigal

✠

# Fr. Len Fecko

**Atonement Retreat Ministry**
**Educational Publications**
**Cincinnati, Ohio**

**armedpublications@icloud.com**

# Acknowledgements

**Cover Artwork:**
Sister Dora Lee Monian, FSCC

**Manuscript and Cover Layout:**
Letty Reifel Hater

**Technology & Marketing Advisor:**
John Fecko

**Business Advisor:**
Bob Dahlheim

**Attitude Adjustment Coordinator:**
Elizabeth Fecko

© 2015  Atonement Retreat Ministry Educational Publications.

ISBN 978-1-5049-7056-3

Printed in the United States

# Introduction

I was having lunch with a group of friends when I announced that I was in the process of writing a book. I passed the draft of the cover design around the table. One of my friends remarked that my proofreader was not very astute because she missed the mistake I made by omitting the word "son" as part of the title. "You are very perceptive," I exclaimed. "But it was not a mistake. You have picked up on the very point I want to make."

The word "prodigal" describes the younger son in the story because he spends money freely or recklessly. But there is another character in the story who fits the definition. This character gives something on a lavish scale and is not concerned about giving it freely or recklessly. This character shows mercy to his lost son; this same character bestows understanding and patience on a lavish scale to his older son. This character, of course, is the father.

The parable provides meaningful lessons for us in several ways. The younger son is the character who reminds us that it is never too late to find our way back to our spiritual home. The older son is the character who reminds us that harboring petty jealousies and judging others with a self-righteous attitude is not the loving way. But it is the father who teaches us about mercy, pardon, forgiveness, and love.

On April 11, 2015, Pope Francis officially proclaimed a "Holy Year of Mercy" which would begin on December 8, 2015, the feast of the Immaculate Conception, and conclude on November 20, 2016, the feast of Christ the King. The Holy Father has called on the Church throughout the world to "refashion itself as a place not of judgment or condemnation but of pardon and merciful love." In **Evangelii Gaudium** Pope Francis emphasizes that "the Church must be a place of mercy, freely given, where everyone can feel welcomed, loved, forgiven and encouraged to live the good life of the Gospel." The Holy Father states that "the church's very credibility is seen in how she shows merciful and compassionate love."

Jubilee years find their origin in the Book of Leviticus (25:8-13) and usually focus on the themes of forgiveness and pardon with the intention of helping people grow closer to God. Jubilee years have been celebrated every twenty-five or fifty years since the 1300's, the last of which was the Jubilee Year of 2000. The Jubilee Year proclaimed by Pope Francis deviates from the 25/50 year cycle and will focus on one of his favorite themes: the mercy of God the Father.

In **Misericordiae Vultus** (The Face of Mercy) the Holy Father explains his rationale for proclaiming the Holy Year: "Perhaps we have long since forgotten how to show and live the way of mercy... mercy is the force that reawakens us to new life and instills in us the courage to look to the future with hope..."

1

Pope Francis continues: "The temptation... to focus exclusively on justice made us forget that this is only the first, albeit necessary and indispensable step..." In proclaiming the Holy Year of Mercy, Pope Francis asserts that "...the time has come for the Church to take up the joyful call to mercy once more."

The Holy Father says that "*Merciful Like the Father*," the motto for the Jubilee Year "...serves as an invitation to follow the merciful example of the Father who asks us not to judge or condemn but to forgive and to give love and forgiveness without measure."

I have followed the news reports announcing the Jubilee Year with keen interest. When I read the reference Pope Francis made to the parable of the prodigal son, his interpretation of the story resonated with me. His statements reminded me of a homily I heard many years ago when I was in high school. Saint Brendan Parish was the neighboring parish to my home parish, Saint Christine, in Youngstown, Ohio. Saint Brendan's had a Sunday evening Mass that attracted high school students from the entire west side of town since it meant that we could sleep in late but still fulfill our Sunday obligation. Father Henry Lileas, the young associate pastor at Saint Brendan, was very popular among high school students. Even though it has been over forty years, I still remember when Father Lileas suggested that perhaps a more appropriate title for the parable was "The Prodigal Father" because he is the one who displays an extravagant display of love for his sons and lavishes them both with mercy and understanding, even though they have treated him poorly.

2

Pope Francis concurs with the interpretation offered by Father Lileas when he says that none of the stories in the scriptures more clearly emphasizes the mercy of God the Father than the parable of the prodigal son **(Luke 15:11-32)**. It is the father who lets his younger son waltz out the door with an inheritance which probably was not rightfully his according ancient Jewish law. Later in the story he goes out in search of the older brother who is refusing to participate in the celebration the father is throwing for his lost brother. This action is another lavish display of love and understanding on the part of the father.

Pope Francis reminds us that Jesus told this parable to help us understand the nature of God the Father. Above and beyond that, Pope Francis emphasizes that Jesus did not merely tell us of the Father's mercy, he says that Jesus himself is the very face of the Father's mercy. He is placing mercy at the very heart of our Christian belief, expressing that mercy is:
• a word which unveils the mystery of the Most Holy Trinity;
• the supreme act by which God comes to meet us;
• the fundamental law that dwells in the heart of every person who looks sincerely into the eyes of his brothers and sisters on the path of life; and
• the bridge that connects God and man, opening our hearts to a hope of being loved forever despite our sinfulness. ("**Misericordiae Vultus**")

During the holy season of Lent, Pope Francis intends to send out priests designated as "Missionaries of Mercy." The Holy Father describes their mission, saying, "They will be a sign of the Church's maternal solicitude for the People of God, enabling them to enter the profound richness of this mystery so fundamental to the faith. There will be priests to whom I will grant the authority to pardon even those sins reserved to the Holy See, so that the breadth of their mandate as confessors will be even clearer. They will be, above all, living signs of the Father's readiness to welcome those in search of His pardon."

Pope Francis has encouraged all bishops and priests, even those who will not be designated as missionaries of mercy to reach out to people with compassion, with the mercy and generosity shown by the father in the beloved parable.

During the Jubilee Year, the cycle of Sunday readings will be taken from the Gospel of Luke, who has traditionally been referred to as the "Evangelist of Mercy." Parables like the lost sheep, the lost coin, and the lost son are all found in Luke's gospel. Pastoral ministers have been encouraged to plan special events and activities during the Jubilee Year to invite the People of God to reflect upon, but even more importantly, to celebrate the abundant mercy of God the Father made incarnate in the person of Jesus Christ, the Son.

Since I am no longer active in full-time parish ministry, I have been wondering what role I might be able to play to be an agent of mercy during the Jubilee Year. That is where the idea of writing a book came to light. This work is my attempt to emphasize the alternative interpretation of the parable that Father Lileas offered years ago, the same interpretation which Pope Francis invites the church to celebrate, as he has proclaimed, "the joy of the Gospel."

*"Throwing aside his cloak,
he jumped up and came to Jesus.
And answering him, Jesus said,
'What do you want me to do for you?'
And the blind man said to Him,
'Rabboni, I want to regain my sight!'
And Jesus said to him,
'Go; your faith has made you well.'
Immediately he regained his sight
and began following Him on the road."* **(Mark 10:51)**

*"Jesus said to her, 'Mary!' She turned and said to Him,
'Rabboni!' (which is to say, Teacher)."*
**(John 20:16)**

      The title *Rabboni* is used only twice in the New Testament, once in the Gospel of Mark **(10:51)** and once in the Gospel of John **(20:16)**. It was a title of Aramaic origin and was used as a Jewish title of respect. It applied especially to spiritual instructors and learned persons. There were three distinct forms of the title, each bestowed upon the masters or teachers with elaborate ceremony.

      The first form of the title was "Rab" and was best translated as "master." This was a Babylonian title given to certain learned men who had received the laying-on of hands in the rabbinic schools. This was the lowest title among the three.

The second form of the title, "Rabbi," meant "my master" or "my teacher." It was a Palestinian designation, where a man was bestowed the title from the laying-on of hands by the Sanhedrin. He was given a key and a scroll when the new title was spoken. The key symbolized that the master possessed the power and authority to teach others, and the scroll symbolized that he was familiar and devoted to his studies. He would wear the key around his neck as a token of greatness, and it was buried with him when he died. A Rabbi was one who had disciples who were prepared to raise up new disciples. This was the second greatest title among the three.

The third form of the title was "Rabbon" meaning "Great Master" or "Rabboni" ("Rabbouni") meaning "My Great Master." This superlative title was the greatest designation of all. Once the teacher had seen two generations of disciples, he was referred to with this title. When this title was used, the teacher was also called by his own name so that he would not be forgotten. Using his name along with the title assumed a deep level of intimacy that the master had with his disciples. The term was not only a title that demonstrated the respect the student had for the teacher, it was also a term of endearment. The Gospel of Luke provides sufficient evidence to show how Jesus fulfilled this requirement. After he chose the twelve, he later appointed another seventy-two, thus fulfilling the requirement for a second generation of disciples.

In the Gospel of Mark, it was a blind man who was *able to see* what others could not: that Jesus was the master teacher, the Rabboni. Although he was *physically blind*, he had the necessary *spiritual vision* to see and understand who Jesus really was. It is unfortunate that many bible translations do not use the superlative title in this particular passage.

In the Gospel of John, it was Mary Magdalene, a woman who had been unfairly judged, criticized by many, and often considered to be a social outcast who was the first to encounter Jesus after his resurrection. In this deeply intimate moment, Mary experienced a revelation about Jesus that no one, not even the disciples, had yet known: he was alive! When Mary addressed Jesus as "Rabboni," she was completing the ritual that began when he was raised from the dead. Mary assumed the role traditionally assumed by the Sanhedrin: she bestowed on Jesus the title of respect. In using the superlative form of the title, Mary displayed her respect and endearment for the Lord and the deep intimacy they shared. It would not be until Thomas cried out, "My Lord and my God" that we will again witness such deep love and respect.

*"After three days they found him in the temple, sitting among the teachers, listening to them and asking questions, and all who heard him were astounded at his understanding and his answers...*
*And Jesus advanced in wisdom and age and in favor with God and man."* **(Luke 3:46-52)**

Some thirty years ago my family spent a week at Walt Disney World in Orlando, Florida. It was a memorable vacation for many reasons, but most importantly because it was the last vacation we shared with my mother before she died. Dad booked a suite at the Contemporary Resort Hotel where the entire family could be together. Since the monorail stopped in the lobby of the hotel, Mom could easily return to the room whenever she was tired. Every morning and every afternoon a buffet was served in the hallway outside our suite. We will always remember that actor Richard Dreyfuss and his family were our neighbors. This was our big claim-to-fame that week!

One of the other stories we share about that special week was the fact that when we went to Epcot Center, one of the things we enjoyed most were the theatre ensembles who performed in various places throughout the park. It is not that we remembered the performances or the actors as much as we remembered the fact that Dad was always chosen to be one of the audience members who would become part of the cast.

One of the special characteristics we loved about Dad was his great sense of humor. He was willing to take part in anything that would make his children and grandchildren smile, even if it meant that he had to subject himself to some good-natured humiliation.

In the world in which Jesus lived, storytelling was a normal pastime activity and one of the primary forms of entertainment, and the best storytellers were dramatic and engaging. I imagine that some storytellers were like the street performers we saw at Epcot Center. Similar dramatic methods would likely have been used in the ancient world.

It goes without saying that Jesus was a master teacher and a master storyteller. He knew how to engage the crowds of people who came from great distances, taking all that into consideration when he began his public ministry.

The life expectancy at the time of Christ was about 47 years for most people. Some did live well into old age, but the high infant and child mortality rates and the lack of sophisticated medical procedures were the reasons why the average life expectancy was considerably lower than it is today.

Tradition tells us that Jesus was likely to be about thirty years old when he began his public ministry. What Jesus may have done for the first thirty years of his life remains a mystery. It was the custom for a young man to follow in the footsteps of his father, which leads us to believe that perhaps Jesus was a carpenter for a time, but we do not know this for certain. One thing we do know for sure, and that is that Jesus developed the ability to be a master storyteller.

It is fascinating to consider what life experiences Jesus had that helped shape him into the master storyteller and master teacher he would later become. I imagine that he took every opportunity to listen to the scholars who might be visiting his hometown of Nazareth. I also believe it is reasonable to assume that he would have participated in any form of spiritual enrichment or educational opportunity that might help him gain wisdom and knowledge.

Most importantly, I imagine that Jesus listened, watched, and observed very carefully. Certainly he paid attention to the way in which people treated one another. He must have been attuned to the level of suffering that people endured; he must have been an eyewitness to the injustices that were imposed upon the weak and lowly, especially women and children; and he must have witnessed first-hand the hatred and prejudices which resulted from a society in which opportunities were closed off to certain people because of social and economic class, family and ethnic origin, and gender. In the way in which the evangelists portray Jesus in the gospels, I think it is evident that he must have taken all these factors into account in his storytelling and teaching, in his healings and miracles, and in the personal encounters he had with people. The early years of his life must have shaped and molded his mind as well as his heart. It is clear in the gospel accounts that Jesus wanted to encourage others to display the same compassion and understanding he had, especially for people who were considered different or who suffered in any way.

I entered the seminary in August, 1984. Although it is well over 30 years now, I vividly remember the first day of the first class that my fellow first-year seminarians and I were required to take. The title of the course was "Biblical Interpretation," and was taught by Father Tim Schehr. Tim is a brilliant scripture scholar and he ranks as one of the most gifted and enthusiastic lecturers I have ever known.

After reviewing the syllabus for the course, Father Tim told us to open our bibles to the first chapter in the Book of Genesis. One barely audible voice surfaced from the back of the classroom communicating the message that most of the students needed to share: "Father, I didn't think that we would need our bibles today." The expression on the Tim's face will be etched in my memory until the day I die. "Gentlemen," he said, "when we study the Holy Scriptures, we need our bibles *every day*." Those words were echoing in our ears when twelve out of fifteen men jumped out of their seats, all scrambling to get back to their rooms to collect their bibles as quickly as possible. All I could do was say a silent prayer, thanking God that I had brought with me the new bible my friend Kyle had given me as a gift when I told her I was entering the seminary. While the three of us who were the remnant of a class of fifteen waited impatiently for the others to return, Father Schehr paced back and forth in the front of the classroom. When he glanced down and saw my new bible, he smiled and said to me, "You don't expect your bible to look so spotless very long, do you?  I can promise you that by the end of this term you will have written dozens of notes in the margins and your bible will have other markings to remind you of pertinent facts."

Although I told Tim that I would not have a problem marking up my bible in this way, I never felt comfortable writing in the holy book.  Instead, I bought a pad of post-a-notes that I keep with my bible at all times.  Whenever I need to write something that will help me in the future, I stick a note in the bible. That gift from my friend became my study bible, and it is now filled with hundreds of slips of paper, scribbled with notes, protruding from the book in every direction.

Father Tim shared a great deal of wisdom with us, but there are two statements of advice that I have always kept in mind when reading the scriptures, especially the parables that Jesus told.  First, he told us to *pay attention to every detail of the story.*  And secondly, he told us that we should *never read more into the story than what the author has included.*  This advice will prove to be significant as we begin to analyze the parable of the prodigal son.

A party game called "Six Degrees of Kevin
Bacon" was dreamed up in 1994 by Craig Fass, Brian
Turtle, and Mike Ginelli, classmates at Albright College
in Reading, Pennsylvania. The game requires players
to link other actors or celebrities to actor Kevin Bacon
of *"Footloose"* fame in as few steps as possible by way
of the movies they have in common. The game was
inspired by s*ix degrees of separation*," the theory that
asserts that nobody is more than six relationships away
from any other person in the world.

We can use this theory in reverse to consider the
differences that exist between the world of the
scriptures and the world in which we live today. The
"degrees of separation" are important when we are
involved in biblical interpretation. If we do not take
them into consideration, we may overlook subtle
details that affect the full meaning of the story.

I would like to suggest six degrees of separation
that are worth considering any time we are attempting
to discover the full meaning of the beloved stories we
find in the gospels.

1.     the intent of the author and the writing style
employed;

2.     the composition of the original audience;

3.     the setting of the story in time and place in
history;

4.    the meaning "within the text" vs. the meaning "behind the text";

5.    the transition from the oral tradition to the written text;  and

6.    the translation and editing from the original language to other languages over time.

I think it is safe to say that most active Christians can recite the story of the prodigal son by heart.  It is one of the best known and beloved of all the parables, yet it worth noting that it is only found in the Gospel of Luke.  Luke's intent is to call upon Christian disciples to identify with the master, Jesus, who is caring and tender toward the poor and lowly, the outcast, the sinner and the afflicted, and toward all those who recognize their dependence on God.  On the other hand, Luke is severe toward the proud and self-righteous, particularly those who place their material wealth before the service of God and neighbor.

As Pope Francis has pointed out, no gospel writer is more concerned than Luke with the mercy and compassion of Jesus.  It is no coincidence, then, that this gospel is identified with the apostle traditionally believed to be a physician.  Stories of healing are a common thread in the Gospel of Luke.

Physicians in the time of Christ did not have extensive academic training, nor did they have access to the sophisticated technology and equipment used by medical practitioners in modern society.  Yet they were nonetheless healers in the truest sense of the word.  They were concerned with the health of the entire person.  Holiness was understood as the well-being of the body, mind, and spirit.  Helping people become "whole or complete" was the essential role of a physician, and the distinction between the physical and the spiritual realms that exists in the world of modern medicine was unheard of in the ancient world. Physicians routinely used balms and salves to treat diseases of the skin and to cure any "dis-ease" of the body, mind, or spirit.

The refrain from one of my favorite African-American Spiritual hymns best expresses this understanding:

"There is a balm in Gilead
that makes the wounded whole;
There is a balm in Gilead that heals a sin sick soul."
(African-American Spiritual, Public Domain)

The theme of inclusion is central to the Gospel of Luke. The "Evangelist of Mercy" is concerned about showing how God's promises to Israel have been fulfilled in Jesus, and how the salvation promised to Israel has been extended to the Gentiles. Another African-American spiritual explains Luke's intent:

"Plenty good room, Plenty good room,
Plenty good room for all God's children;
Plenty good room, Plenty good room,
Choose your seat and sit down."
(African-American Spiritual, Public Domain)

Storytelling has always been a marvelous way to open the minds of people to new ways of thinking and understanding, and open their hearts to new ways of acceptance and love. Therefore, it makes sense that there are more parables included in the Gospel of Luke than any of the other gospels. There are 13 parables in Mark, 29 in Matthew, and 37 in Luke. The Gospel of

John is unique and has only two parable-like images: the shepherd and sheep and the vine and the branches.

The use of parables as a storytelling method or as a style of writing is used when the author wants the audience or reader to be fully engaged in the discovery process. Parables do not define things precisely as lectures are designed to do, but rather they use comparisons to describe some aspect of how things are related to one another. In the case of the parables that Jesus told, they describe how God acts in history and interacts with human beings. Most parables contain some elements within the story that seem strange or unusual, especially to the original audience. Parables can be as simple as the simile-style used in the Gospel of John ("I am the vine; you are the branches") (15:5) or as complex as the parable of the Sower and the Seed (Matt. 13:1-23, Mark 4:3-9 and Luke 8:1-15) in which case Jesus takes the time to explain the meaning of the images of the seed to the twelve apostles after the crowd has dispersed.

The parables found in the gospels often include an element of surprise so that the listeners or readers can see themselves in the story or discover how God relates to them. This is why it is important to pay attention to the audience to whom Jesus is speaking when he is teaching in parables. Is it the disciples, the crowds, or as so often the case, the scribes and Pharisees? In the Gospel of Luke we discover at the beginning of Chapter 13 who the audience is:

"The tax collectors and sinners were all drawing near to listen to him, but the Pharisees and scribes began to complain, saying,

'This man welcome sinners and eats with them.'
So to them he addressed this parable..."
*(Luke 13:1)*

We know from this introductory sentence that
the crowd that had gathered was composed of many
different people, but Jesus is addressing the story to
the scribes and Pharisees in particular. Jesus first tells
the parable of the lost sheep, then the parable of the
lost coin, and finally the parable of the lost son. We
can use our imagination to visualize how Jesus may
have slowly walked up to the group of scribes and
Pharisees who were mumbling among themselves, and
we can also picture in our minds how the rest of the
crowd may have pressed in so that they could hear
every word that the master was about to say. I doubt
that any of them walked away. They would have been
listening more intently than ever!

Perhaps the best reason for using parables as a
style of storytelling or writing is because parables force
the listeners or readers to think! Parables remind us
that the Word of God is alive and has as much meaning
for us today as it did for our ancestors in faith.
Parables teach us that there may be a variety of
meanings found within the stories.

The time and place in history as well as the
cultural norms are also important factors to consider
whenever we are attempting to discover the complete
and complex meaning of a story. Pastor Ron Redder,
my first homiletics professor, emphasized this fact
when he encouraged us to always begin our homilies
by "setting the scene" for the scripture passage that we
would refer to in our homilies. The historical and

cultural factors that were important to the original audience may differ from those of the readers of the story at later periods in history. Comparing what was going on "then" with what is going on "now" is a fascinating way to see how the Word of God transcends time and culture.

I attended a fascinating lecture at the 2004 Los Angeles Religious Education Congress. Father Felix Just, S.J., Executive Director of the Loyola Institute for Spirituality in Orange, CA, used the example of the Parable of the Sower and the Seed **(Matthew 13:1-23, Mark 4:3-9 and Luke 8:1-15)** as way of explaining how there may be meaning found "behind the text" as well as the meaning that is found "within the text."

In the parable of the Sower and the Seed, the meaning found "within the text" is simple enough to understand since Jesus later provides a detailed explanation to the apostles. To uncover the meaning found "behind the text" we have to delve more deeply into the passage, paying attention to every detail included in the story.

Fr. Just pointed out the fact that the farmer seemed to be quite careless when he was sowing his seed. After all, some seed fell on the path and was trampled; some seed fell on rocky ground and never had a chance take root; and some seed fell among the thorns and was strangled. In the three cases mentioned, the seed was lost. In the world of abundance in which we live, we may read this story without giving a second thought to the farmer's carelessness. But in ancient times, seed was not very plentiful, and what was available was usually very expensive, especially for individual farmers. The original audience would have been taken by surprise when they heard this detail of the story. We can imagine how the members of the audience might have turned to one another in amazement or disbelief. We can imagine that someone in the crowd would have voiced aloud what the others were thinking: "*What an idiot!*" or "*You've got to be kidding me!*"

We know that Jesus will later explain to the apostles what the seed that fell on the path, the seed that fell on the rocky ground, and the seed that fell among the thorns represented. But the detail of the farmer's carelessness was simply something that was unheard of in the world in which Jesus lived. The audience would never let this detail pass without wondering why the farmer could be so careless. As Fr. Just suggested, there *must* be a reason why Jesus included the detail of the farmer's apparent wastefulness, and that reason is to talk about the *abundance of love* possessed by God the Father, represented, of course, by the Sower. The Father is the Sower of divine love! The Father has an abundance of seed to give, and wastefulness is not His concern. While human love may have limits, the love of God is plentiful and unconditional. It can be lavishly extended without concern for wastefulness. This motif extends throughout Luke's writings as Jesus continues to describe the nature of His Father to the scribes and Pharisees (as well as the tax collectors and sinners) when he tells the story of the lost son: the *prodigal* display of love God the Father bestows on his children.

*Sitz im Leben* is the German term used by scripture scholars to take into consideration the meaning "within the text" as well as the meaning "behind the text". The social context or "life setting" of a particular passage or story includes the historical, cultural and sociological context in which the author lived and wrote. These are important factors to keep in mind when we are trying to determine the complete meaning which the author is trying to convey.

The changes that may have been made in the transition from the story being told in the oral tradition to the written text may limit the reader from appreciating the voice inflection of the storyteller, the emphasis the original storyteller may have placed on certain words or phrases, and the tone of voice that may have been used to convey meaning. The choice of words or phrases and other editing decisions that may have been made as the story was translated from the original language to other languages might also result in loss of meaning or a loss of various interpretations of the story.

In the English speaking world, many Catholics, or to be more specific, many priests in the Archdiocese of Cincinnati, still struggle with the 2011 translation of the Roman Missal. The committee that was responsible for the new translation may have been composed of brilliant Latin scholars, but their understanding of the English language (with its many forms throughout the English speaking world) may leave something to be desired. Some of the phrasing and the words that were chosen seem rather archaic, at least in the United States. Priests have been advised to read ahead so that we will not be surprised by the phrasing that is used or stumble on many of the six syllable words that may bring points in a *Scrabble* game, but are rarely used in everyday conversation.

The changes that have occurred over time in the scriptures because of different translations do not affect most of us on a daily basis. We are able to read a passage from the scriptures, and through the process of prayer and reflection, we can determine for ourselves what meaning the passage has for us in our lives. But sometimes the choices made by an editor or translator to use a particular word or phrase may have an impact on the interpretation of the passage. As we will see in the case of the parable of the lost son, sometimes these differences can limit our understanding of a passage or prohibit us from appreciating the subtle messages or multiple meanings the story might have.

Father John DeMarinis was the Dean of Men at
Ursuline High School.  He was also my sophomore home
room teacher and religion teacher.  His hands-on style of
discipline was accepted during the baby boomer era.  A rap
on the head using his knuckles or a squeeze in the muscle
of the neck or shoulder blade were common ways he used
to get the attention of male students.  Many guys in our
school also witnessed his "foot-on" style of discipline that
demonstrated his ability to walk up or down the steps while
at the same time kicking the posterior end of a
misbehaving adolescent, never missing a step or a kick.
The truth is that these scenes were not very common.  My
guess is that Fr. DeMarinis did this once or twice at the
beginning of the school year to instill fear into the minds
and hearts of the first year students.  "Dee-Mo," as he was
affectionately called, was known more for his bark than his
bite.  His booming voice gained our full attention.  He also
had a penchant for choosing unusual words or phrases to
make a point.  Some of these, I am certain, he created
himself.  The word I remember Fr. DeMarinis using most
often was the word "***rumdum,***" but perhaps it was the way
he said this word that was most memorable.

Rumdum was always proceeded by the word "you."
It was "you rumdum" when he was speaking to one student
and "you rumdums" when he was speaking to an entire
class.  Father stretched out the word "you" similar to the

way baseball umpires stretch out the word "strike" when calling balls and strikes.  All of this created a very dramatic effect, and anyone who was within hearing distance came to full attention whenever Fr. DeMarinis called someone a rumdum.

The dictionary describes a rumdum as "a drunkard or a derelict alcoholic."  The meaning of the word transposes all languages and requires no translation.  If you correctly use the DeMarinis tone of voice, it does not matter if you call another person a rumdum in Italian or Spanish, French or German, Polish or Russian, Japanese or Chinese, and maybe in Klingon, they will understand that you are putting them down, and it doesn't matter whether or not they have had a drop to drink!

There is no word I can think of that better describes the sons in Luke's parable.  We will focus our attention on the older son later, but for now, the best way to begin our reflection of the parable is by concentrating on the younger son.

Anyone who has seen the Broadway play or the film version of "*Fiddler on the Roof*" knows that tradition was very important in the ancient Jewish culture. Traditions, norms, and laws set forth the appropriate behavior in everything from religious worship to options for career choices. For example, we know that in the ancient Jewish tradition, only men who were from the line of Aaron could become priests. "*Fiddler on the Roof*" touched the hearts of millions because it addressed the strict traditions that limited the options available to women in that time and culture.

Traditions and laws also set forth the appropriate ways of behaving and interacting within the family. A person's status within the family, within the religious community, and within the economic system, all depended on the person's relationship to the head of the household, the father. Not only was he the leader of the family, his wife and children were considered to be his possessions. From the time of Moses, religious commandments served as the basis for this patriarchal system. Children were taught from a very early age to honor both father and mother, but disrespecting the father was viewed as a sufficient reason for imposing extreme disciplinary action on the child, going as far as disowning or ostracizing the child by the entire family.

Ancient Jewish law also set forth the way in which wealth and property was passed on from one generation to another.  There was a strict system of *primogeniture* which emphasized the relationship each family member had to the male head of the household.  When the father died, the entire inheritance would be passed on to the oldest son. Daughters and younger sons would inherit nothing.  In fact, aside from a few family heirlooms and sentimental keepsakes, the wife inherited nothing.  It would be the responsibility of the eldest son to care for his mother for the rest of her life, but he was the one who would inherit whatever fortune the family might have, as well as the family's property and the family business.  The eldest son might include his brothers as partners in the family business, but we know from the Old Testament story of Joseph and his brothers that there were also cases of jealousy and rivalry.

Keeping all this in mind, we can easily imagine the reaction of the crowd as Jesus begins to tell his story.

A man had two sons, and the younger son said to his father,
"Father, give me the share
of your estate that should come to me."
So the father divided the property between them.

I imagine that everyone who was listening to Jesus would have been astounded when they heard the young son's request. In the first place, it was simply unimaginable for a son to ask his father for his inheritance while the father was still alive. The son was displaying behavior which showed ultimate disrespect for his father. In the second place, his request makes no sense. Since he is the younger son, he would not inherit anything. It is likely that Jesus' audience would have expected the father to react by rending or tearing his garments. The ancient ritual of rending or tearing of garments represented mourning, namely, on account of some important truth having been destroyed, or because there was no faith. The younger son was completely ignoring the laws governing inheritance and the customary respect that should be shown to the father. The response the crowd expected to hear from the father would be something like this:

"So you want your share of the inheritance?
I will give you your share of the inheritance.
In fact, I will give you seven times
your share of the inheritance.
You Rumdum! Seven times zero is Zero!"

That would have been the response of any good, respectable Jewish father of the time. Instead, the father did just as the younger son requested. Using a formula not explained in the story, he managed to divide the estate into two parts, sold half off, and gave the money to his son.

I cannot emphasize enough how important it is to always keep in mind what the reaction of the original audience might have been. In a culture in which norms and traditions were so important, the listeners must have been looking at one another in disbelief, wondering whether Jesus had lost his mind. But we know that Jesus is demonstrating his skill as a master storyteller. He has just begun to tell the story, and already he must have had the audience's undivided attention!

After a few days, the younger son collected
all his belongings and set off to a distant country where he
squandered his inheritance on a life of dissipation.

We are not provided with specific details as to what a life of dissipation might have been in ancient times, but it is safe to say that it was not much different than what it is in our time. In contemporary language, we might say that the young man spent all the money his father had given him on wine, women and song.

And then famine came on that land.
And he found himself in dire need.
So he hired himself out to one of the local citizens
who sent him to his farm to tend the swine.
And he longed to eat the fill of the pods
on which the swine fed, but nobody gave him any.

This particular passage is an excellent example of why it is important to keep in mind the "degrees of separation" relevant in biblical interpretation. Jesus was addressing this story to Jewish scribes and Pharisees. And in the story, we are told that a young Jewish man is tending pigs. Even people with limited knowledge of the Jewish religion know that pigs are not kosher. Strict dietary laws forbade Jewish people from eating them, even if they were starving. The young man has hit rock bottom, envying the slop thrown to non-kosher animals. In a Jewish story, you can't get any lower than that!

Coming to his senses he thought,
"How many of my father's hired workers
Have more than enough food to eat,
but here am I, dying from hunger."

This passage provides another example of how the degrees of separation influence the meaning of a story. Scripture scholars and historians generally agree that the language spoken by Jesus was Aramaic. When the shift from the oral tradition to the written tradition occurred, Greek was the language most commonly used. In the fourth century, Saint Jerome translated the Greek into Latin. Later in history, Latin was translated into every language used throughout the world. In every step in this process, choices made by translators have affected the way in which the story has been interpreted. For example, the NAB translation says, *"coming to his senses"*, but the phrase in Greek is more closely translated as *"he said to himself"* and can be interpreted in two ways: 1.) *"realizing the situation"* or 2.) *"coming to his true self, his sane mind."* These subtle differences have lead to different interpretations of why he made the decision to return home.

Luke makes no specific mention of a change of heart and thus various interpretations have been suggested. Many scholars assert that some conversion must have taken place. Others believe that the young man has simply realized that there is a Plan B available to him, and that is to go home for a good meal. A third school of scholarly thought says that is very possible that both meanings are intended. The young man finally understood that there was no hope for him in that distant land, and the fond memories of his home and father changed his way of thinking (one of the first steps necessary in a conversion experience). I am told that one of the Greek words used in this passage is found only in the New Testament. It refers to the love and affection shared in the home by a father and his children, and this love and affection is provided to excess. There is more love and affection there than can ever be used.

Later in the story we will see how this idea once again comes to light in the interaction between the father and the eldest son. It also provides us with a clue as to which character was the most "prodigal" in the sense of demonstrating a lavish display or giving in an extravagant way or to excess.

I shall get up and go to my father and I shall say to him, "Father, I have sinned against heaven and against you. I no longer deserve to be called your son; treat me as you would treat one of your hired workers."

When reading this passage, I am reminded of the advice given by Father Tim Schehr: *do not read more into the story than what the author has provided.* Although this beloved parable has been used as a starting point to talk about conversion, in this particular passage the young man seems to be scripting a prepared statement the same way a lawyer prepares a witness to testify so that the jury will rule in the client's favor. It takes a far stretch of the imagination to believe that the son experienced anything resembling conversion. There does not seem to be a tone of sincerity in his statement to his father.

Although scripture scholars have debated this point for generations, it seems to me that this young man is doing nothing more than planning his next ploy as a con artist so that he can take advantage of his father one more time. He was able to convince his father to give him an inheritance that was not rightly his, and now he is plotting his next move so that his father will let him return home. As far as we can tell, this young man was a selfish, self-centered rumdum at the beginning of the story, and he is a selfish, self-centered rumdum at the end of the story!

So he got up and went back to his father.

In any case, the young man finds his way home. We can imagine the reaction of the crowd when Jesus said that he went back to his father. I can picture them rubbing their hands together, saying to one another, "This is going to be good!" It is likely that they were anticipating a dramatic response from the father when the young son showed up. I know that if I would have pulled a stunt like this when I was young, I would have been dreading the reaction of my Dad.

*While he was still a long way off, his father*
*caught sight of him, and was filled with compassion.*
*He ran to his son, embraced him and kissed him.*

This was certainly not the reaction Jesus' audience was anticipating. The father has not disowned his son as they had expected. Instead, the father is filled with compassion when he sees his son "coming from a distance." This is another detail in the story which is often overlooked. If the father caught sight of the son while he was still a long way off, this suggests that he had been waiting and watching for him. This suggests that he may have been grieving ever since his son left.

Then Jesus says something that would have definitely shocked his audience: the father *ran* to his son. A rabbi once told me that in the ancient Jewish culture, older Jewish men did not run, especially towards a disrespectful child. A well-respected Jewish father would have taken his place at the seat of honor and waited for the child to humbly appear before him as a sign of respect. But that is not what happened in this story. Instead, the father responds with a lavish display of love and affection. Even after the young son played him and treated him as a fool in public, the father runs to his son and embraces and kisses him! The father is not concerned about his son's disrespectful behavior. He is not concerned with what other people might think of him. He is filled with joy because his lost son has returned.

If I had been the son who had been away from home for a long period of time, my father might have embraced me when I returned, but immediately thereafter, he would have done what Jesus' listeners would have expected any

31

good [Jewish] parent to do, and that is to demand answers
to questions such as these:

**"Are you alright?"**

**"What have you been doing?"**

**"Why are your clothes so filthy?"**

**"Why are you dressed that way?"**

**"Why do you smell like a filthy animal?"**

**"Why are you so thin?"**

And most importantly,

**"Where is the family money I gave you?"**

But nothing like that happened in this story.
Instead, the son begins to recite what appears to be the
script he rehearsed during his journey home:

"Father, I have sinned against heaven and against you;
I no longer deserve to be called your son."

Only the original audience would have known
whether the young son was sincere because they had the
good fortune in being able to hear the tone of voice that
Jesus used as he described the son's response. If this scene
was performed by a group of actors today, their body
language, their physical movements, and the tone of their
voices could be used as a way of suggesting various ways of
interpreting the son's sincerity. The creative ingenuity of
an author is exhibited whenever an opportunity is provided
for the reader to use imagination and personal insight.
This story clearly proves that Luke was the recipient of
divine inspiration.

But his father ordered his servants,
"Quickly bring the finest robe and put it on him;
put a ring on his finger and sandals on his feet.
Take the fattened calf and slaughter it.
Then let us celebrate with a feast..."

*"Unimaginable!"* *"Not in my lifetime!"* These were phrases I imagine were uttered by the people who were listening to Jesus as he told this incredible story. Everything that was part of their culture and tradition was being called into question. A robe was given to an honored guest, a ring signified authority, and only family members wore sandals. Yet the father is giving these items to a disrespectful son who should have been disowned. This was definitely not the way things happened in their world. If the purpose of a parable is to surprise the audience, there is no question that the people who were listening to Jesus were surprised!

"...this son of mine was dead, and has come to life again;
he was lost, and has been found."
Then the celebration began.

This passage has also been used by some scholars to support the theory that the young man did have a conversion experience. But note that it is the father who is speaking. Even though he would have been within his rights to say to his son, "You are dead to me" he announces to his servants that his son has "come to life again." He does not view their relationship as broken or destroyed.

The fact of the matter is that it is irrelevant whether or not the son experienced conversion, a change of heart, or metanoia. By this time, it should be clear that the son is not the central character in this story.  Jesus wants his audience to pay attention to the father and the *prodigal*, recklessly extravagant response he exhibits.  If the interaction between the father and the younger son was not enough to emphasize this point, Jesus now goes on to describe the interaction the father has with his older son.

Now the older son had been out in the field
And on his way back, as he neared the house,
He heard the sound of music and dancing.
He called one of the servants and asked what this might mean.
The servant said to him, "Your brother has returned and your
father  has slaughtered the fattened calf
because he has him back safe and sound."

Scripture scholars tell us that in Greek, the servant's response is filled with sarcasm.  Unfortunately, that subtlety does not translate well into English, and therefore we are left with another degree of separation.  The point is, even the servants think the father is not behaving rationally. Once again, Jesus, the master storyteller, is making an incredible impression on his audience.

He became angry; when he refused to enter the house,
his father came out and pleaded with him.

The older son refuses to go inside and join in the celebration.  Once again, we have a detail of the story that is often overlooked.  In the ancient Jewish world, it would have been considered disrespectful for a son to refuse to sit down at table with his father and break bread, no matter who was present at the table. Once again, Jesus is describing to his audience what, in their minds, would have been unthinkable behavior.  The older son may not have been a total rumdum like his brother, but the description of his behavior would have certainly raised an eyebrow among Jesus' listeners.

The Father's reaction is what we should expect at this point.  He is the one who humbles himself and comes out to plead with his oldest son to come inside and join in the celebration.

He said to his father in reply,
"Look, all these years I served you
and not once did I disobey your orders;
yet you never gave me even a young goat
to feast on with my friends.
But when your son returns who swallowed
up your property with prostitutes,
for him you slaughter the fattened calf."

The oldest son responds the way siblings have responded for countless generations, by crying out in frustration, *"It's not fair!"*  Parents who have more than one child have undoubtedly heard this cry dozens of times, and anyone like me who has brothers or sisters would be lying if they told you they never cried out in this way to gain sympathy from their mom or dad.

The older son thinks the issue is all about justice.  And if it is about justice, then yes, the father may be acting unjustly.  Many other gospel stories talk about justice, but not this one.  This is a story about the *prodigal behavior* of the father who lavishly bestows an extravagant amount of love, mercy and compassion on his children.

He said to him,
"My son, you are here with me always;
everything I have is yours."

    The father does not refute anything his oldest son said regarding his loyalty or his brother's indiscretions. Instead, he reminds him that everything he has is his. The older son could have argued that it was 50% less thanks to his brother's shenanigans, but once again, this points to the fact that the father has such an abundant amount to give, that even 50% of the original inheritance would have been a fortune. The understanding of the father's excess and extravagance is central to this story. Perhaps this is why the father does not address the issue of justice. Justice is important and may be wonderful, but justice is only part of agape, the endless and perfect self-gift of love. Agape is what the father is trying to convey to his sons, and agape is what Jesus is trying to convey to his listeners when he is talking about His Father.

But now we must celebrate and rejoice,
because your brother was dead and has come to life again;
he was lost and has been found."

    This brings us to the great moment, the understanding of what this parable is all about. It is not a parable about forgiveness. It is not a story about conversion. It is a story about the *incomprehensible goodness of God.* The parable of the prodigal son is not a story about the sons. It is not a story about us (although it a story *for* us). It is a story about the Father who loves us, the Father who has *always* loved us and *will always love*

36

*us*, the Father who has always and will always give us the free, self-gift of love.  God loves us unconditionally.  God loves us without expecting anything in return.  It does not matter how many distant lands we have wandered through, and it does not matter how we have squandered the good fortune we have received on a life of debauchery.  If we, like the lost son, are somehow able to find our way back, the Father will be there, waiting and watching, ready to embrace us, reminding us how much we are loved.

I can never read this parable without thinking about the encounter Jesus had with the woman at the well: *"Come, see a man who told me everything I ever did..."* **(John 4:29).**  The Father knows us.  He knows everything we have ever done.   He knows the worst of our sins (represented by the younger son), and He knows the petty thoughts we have and the small-minded judgments we make when we compare ourselves to others (represented by the oldest son). And yet, knowing everything about us, He loves us.

In telling this parable, Jesus was providing his audience with a very powerful image of His Father.  He could have easily begun the parable by saying to the tax collectors and sinners, as well as to the scribes and Pharisees, "Let me tell you about my Dad..."

The Gospel parables help us see ourselves in the stories, perhaps as one of the characters, or by helping us relate to the story from a personal experience.  In either case, the stories challenge us to make changes in our behavior or our way of life.

As a way of concluding my reflection on the parable of the lost son, I would like to share three stories from my life which have helped me understand  the message Jesus was trying to convey.  First, they have helped me better understand the nature of God the Father.  Secondly, the stories have helped me understand what it means to be truly sorry and have a change of heart - in short, to experience conversion or metanoia.  These stories are in my mind, excellent examples of why Pope Francis has invited the Church throughout the world to celebrate a Holy Year of Mercy.

## The Nature of the Father

"*Of the Father's Love Begotten*" is one of my favorite Christmas carols. This beautiful hymn, written by Marcus Aurelius Clemens Prudentius, is rooted in the theology of the Trinity. The words of the first stanza poetically describe Jesus as the source and the eternal expression of the Father's love.

*"He is Alpha and Omega,*
*He the source, the ending He"*

In what I now refer to as "The Parable of the Prodigal," we can begin to understand God as being the fullest expression of love and mercy. If we believe we are made in the image and likeness of God, then the challenge we face is to allow God's divine nature to permeate our total being so that others will see God in us. Although our human nature limits our capacity to become the fullest expression of God to others, when we come close, our souls should leap for joy.

I know that my limitations outweigh my capacity for this fullest expression of love, but there have been a few times in my life when I can humbly say that I did allow the divine nature that is in me to burst forth. The first story I would like to share is a remembrance of one of these special occasions.

One Sunday in the spring of 1979, my family came to visit me to help me put the final decorative touches in my new apartment. The two features that I liked best about this apartment were the screened-in lanai that overlooked a beautiful pond and the huge master bedroom. My parents bought me a plant stand as a house-warming gift which filled one corner of the bedroom, adding both color and charm. The plant stand had eight shelves on which I placed potted plants. At the top, decorative hooks extended outwards which were designed to hang more plants from macramé hangers. Mom knew how to macramé, so she made the hangers, and my sister, Joyce, made all the ceramic pots for the plants.

After lunch the adults decided to sit and visit on the lanai. My oldest niece, Stephanie, who was three years old at the time, had no interest in sitting and listening to the adults. Stephanie always carried a collection of Barbie dolls, stuffed animals, and Cabbage Patch Kids with her. She also insisted on packing a small cassette player and a few cassette tapes. Although she had never seen the film, the songs from the musical, "Grease," were some of her favorites. I told her she could use the boom box in my bedroom so the music would sound better. She was more than happy to take her dolls and plush friends into the bedroom and listen to her music.

The adults were enjoying our visit and everything seemed to be going fine. But soon the sounds from the bedroom grew louder. Stephanie was listening to her favorite song, 'Greased Lightnin'. "Oh my," Joyce sighed, "she always gets wound up when this song is playing. I better check to make sure she is not getting too wild." Joyce was seven months pregnant at the time, so it took her longer than usual to get up from the chaise lounge she was sitting on. But before she put her glass of limeade on the table, we heard a loud crash. Instantly, we knew what had happened: Stephanie was dancing around the room, not realizing how close she was to the plant stand, and as she swung her arms, one of her toys smashed into it. Before we could run from the lanai to the bedroom, the door opened. Olivia Newton-John and John Travolta were still singing as Stephanie appeared, looking directly but sheepishly towards me, tears already streaming down her face. She knew that she had done something wrong. And she knew that her Mamma had made the beautiful ceramic pots that crashed onto the floor, breaking into dozens of pieces.

As soon as I saw the look on my niece's face, I knew that there were no powers in heaven or on earth that had the force to  prevent me from doing anything but picking up my precious niece and holding her in my arms, embracing her with love. The passage from scripture that always comes to mind when I remember that day long ago is from Paul's letter to the Romans. Paul tells us that nothing can separate us from the love of Christ. And nothing can separate us from the love the Father has for us, the kind of love that Jesus was describing when he told the story of the lost son.  It is intrinsic to God's nature, within the very core of God's being, to reach out to us, even when we have done wrong - especially when we have seriously sinned - to embrace us and hold us softly and tenderly in his arms, completely enfolding us with compassion, mercy, and love.

## A Case of True Conversion

For generations scripture scholars have argued whether or not the lost son experienced conversion. Although the case can be made for or against his change of heart, it really does not matter if we shift the focus of our attention on the father instead of the son. The following story is an example of a lost son who found his way and really did experience a complete change of heart.

One summer many years ago, two of my friends and I decided to take advantage of the long Fourth of July holiday weekend to visit our friend, Alice, who lived in a city on the East Coast. A few days before we were scheduled to depart, Alice called to ask me if I would be willing to preside at the Sunday evening Mass at the maximum security prison where she served as chaplain. The priest who was scheduled to preside that evening cancelled because he had an opportunity to visit his family for the holiday weekend.

We had an early dinner on Sunday so that we could arrive in plenty of time for Mass. We planned to stop somewhere on the way home for dessert. When we arrived at the men's prison, a large multi-purpose room was set up for the celebration. The sounds of piano, trumpets, guitars, and bongo drums accompanied the incredible choir that included voices of both guards and prisoners. By the time the prelude music was over, we knew that this was going to be a very lively celebration!

After the entrance hymn and the opening rites, we sat down to listen to the readings from the Scriptures. The Old Testament passage was read by one of the guards, and the New Testament passage was read by one of the prisoners. I will never forget this young man as long as I live. When he walked up to the ambo, he looked like a young adult I expected to see walking across the campus of the University of Cincinnati where I was a campus minister, not in a maximum security prison. And let me tell you, this young man did not simply read the Scriptures, he **proclaimed** the Word of God! Unfortunately, we were not permitted to have any interaction with the prisoners after Mass, so I never had the opportunity to talk to him.

As soon as we sat down at the table in the restaurant on our way home, one of my friends asked Alice, "Who was that handsome young man, and what is he doing in prison?" Then Alice shared one of the most amazing stories we ever heard.

The young man was born out of wedlock. The only time his biological father visited was when he needed money. When he did show up, he was either drunk or high, and he usually got into an argument with the boy's mother which often resulted in a scuffle with his son. Time after time he told the young boy that he was worthless and would never amount to anything.

The boy's mother was not much of a role model either. She was out almost every night, and she rarely got up in the morning to make certain that her son had breakfast before heading off to school. Child services had been called into the home quite frequently, but somehow

43

the woman managed to maintain custody of her son. When she would get angry with him, she would tell him that he was not even worth the welfare money she received for him. When she got really drunk, she would tell him that she would have been better off if she had taken the advice of his father and had an abortion.

The boy was smart, but he was always a disciplinary problem at school. His teachers admitted that even though he should have been held back because of excessive absences, he was routinely promoted to the next grade simply because he would then become another teacher's problem. He learned very quickly that good looks and charm were attributes he possessed that would get him whatever he wanted from most people. In high school, he always managed to have girlfriends who would write his papers and do his homework for him. He had no interest in going to college or joining the military after high school. He had a part-time job at an auto mechanic shop, so he decided to work there full time after graduation. The young woman who became his serious girlfriend planned to go to a college away from home.

One night during the Christmas holidays, the couple went to a party that was being hosted by one of their high school friends. The young woman went into the kitchen to get drinks, and while she was there, she ran into a young man who was in some of her classes at college. They knew they were from the same hometown, but they went to different high schools. They were discussing the friends they had in common when the young man came into the kitchen. He assumed that they were having a relationship at college, so he started mouthing off to the other young man. One thing led to another. Soon there was pushing and shoving.  The young man looked down and saw a knife on the kitchen counter.  He picked it up and stabbed the other young man in the throat, killing him instantly.  At nineteen years of age, he was sent to prison for life.  The reason he did not receive the death penalty was the fact that the murder was not premeditated.

Alice told us that when he first arrived at the prison, his attitude was horrible. He continued to use people in any way he could to get the things he wanted.  About a year later, Alice noticed that the young man had signed up to participate in one of the bible studies that she scheduled periodically for the prisoners.  She told us she considered telling the young man that he was not permitted to attend, but then she realized this was not the Christian way, especially considering the fact that she was the chaplain! Instead, she told him that he could attend as long as he was not disruptive.  The young man showed up for the bible study, but he sat in the back of the room by himself, never participating in the discussion. Alice knew that in prison, it is better to sign up for any activity than to sit in a cell alone.

Two years later something amazing happened. Instead of sitting in the back of the room, the young man sat with the other bible study participants.  Eventually he began to take part in the discussions, and over time, he began asking Alice more questions about Jesus. The next year, the young man asked if he could become part of the RCIA program, the formation program for adults wishing to be baptized or confirmed in the Catholic faith.  He had never set foot in a church his entire life, but he decided that he wanted to be baptized.

Three other men were to be baptized at the Easter Vigil that year.  This was the first time that any of the prisoners had asked to be baptized, so Alice wanted to make the celebration very special.  She asked the warden if the prisoners and guards could work together to create a large baptismal font.  Her plan was to use one of the plastic pool inserts that are often used for landscaping.  The warden told Alice that he and his wife had a swimming pool that they brought with them from their former home, thinking they would install it in their backyard that summer. It was stored in their garage, but he said he was willing to donate it for the Easter celebration.  What he did not tell her was that this pool was so large that it filled the entire garage.  The warden was Baptist, and in the Baptist tradition, people are submerged into the water when they are baptized, so this is why he thought his pool was the perfect size.  Alice was surprised when the pool was delivered, but she was glad that they would have a baptismal font worth remembering!

The prisoners and guards worked together to build steps so that those who would be baptized could easily step into the water.  Alice was anxious because none of the priests who regularly helped out at the prison was available to preside at the Easter Vigil, but somehow the Holy Spirit provided.  Alice had a neighbor whose brother was the abbot of a nearby monastery. He planned to spend Easter with his family, so he volunteered to preside at the Easter Vigil.  When Alice called to talk to him about the details for the celebration and told him about the super sized baptismal font, he laughed and told her that he would bring a change of clothes, including a second alb, so that he could go into the water with the men who would be baptized.

And that is precisely what happened. When it came time for the baptism, the four prisoners stripped down to their boxer shorts.  The abbot was wearing sandals, so he followed the men into the water.  The young man was the last one to be baptized.  The abbot knew nothing of this young man's story, so Alice said she was absolutely convinced that the Holy Spirit was at work when she witnessed what happened.  The abbot held the young man's chest with one arm and pushed his face into the water with the other, saying to him, "I baptize you in the name of the Father ..."  For some reason, however, the abbot held this young man's face in the water until he began to struggle to come up for air.  The abbot let go for just a second so that the young man could catch his breath.  Then he pushed him into the water a second time, saying, "and of the Son...".  He let go a second time, but quickly pushed the young man's head under the water a third time, saying, "and of the Holy Spirit."  But this time the abbot held young man under the water even longer, so that he was literally fighting to come to the surface for air.  When the abbot finally let go, the young man came out of the water, gasping for air.  Alice told us she knows in her heart that she witnessed this young man receiving the breath of the Holy Spirit in the new life of baptism.

Alice said that what happened next was even more incredible.  By the look on his face, Alice could tell that the young man realized what had just happened.  All his sins had been washed away through the waters of baptism!  His emotions overpowered him, and he burst into tears, falling into the arms of the abbot.  "There he was," Alice described, "soaking wet and almost completely naked, sobbing uncontrollably, holding on to the abbot for dear life, dear *new life*!"  It did not matter that he would probably spend the rest of his life in prison.  And even though he could never take away the hurt that he caused in the lives of so many people, at this moment in his life, this young man believed what Alice had taught him: through the power of the Sacrament of Baptism, all his sins were washed away.

Alice told us that she never knew how long the young man held on to the abbot. She said she does remember one thing: except for the young man's sobs, there was not a sound in the room. Everyone was absorbed in this Kairos moment. It was God's time!

Pope Francis says, "Jesus affirms that mercy is not only an action of the Father, it becomes a criterion for ascertaining who His true children are. In short, we are called to show mercy because mercy has first been shown to us." The Holy Father says that in many scripture passages, "justice is understood as the full observance of the Law... in conformity with God's commandments." "Mercy and justice," he says, "are not two contradictory realities, but two dimensions of a single reality that unfolds progressively until it culminates in the fullness of love." In the Gospel of Matthew, Jesus clearly explains how love is the fullest expression of the law. When asked which commandment is greatest in the Law, he responds by saying:

"Love the Lord your God with all your heart
and with all your soul and with all your mind.
This is the first and greatest commandment.
And the second is like it:
'Love your neighbor as yourself.
All the Law and the Prophets
hang on these two commandments."
**-Matthew 22:34-40**

The final story I wish to share is an example of the culmination of mercy and justice and the best example I have ever witnessed that is the fullest expression of agape, the endless and perfect love that the Father shares with Jesus, the Son, and which Jesus, in turn, wants to share with us.

As seminarians we were required to complete the basic unit in Clinical Pastoral Education (CPE) in order to be certified as a hospital chaplain. Four of us had the opportunity to spend a summer in the Boston area while we completed our training at a cancer research hospital.

I became friends with a woman who came to the hospital for radiation and chemotherapy treatments. Unfortunately, none of the treatments stopped the cancer from spreading throughout her entire body. Eventually she was admitted into the hospice wing of the hospital.

One of the things we learned about each other was that we both enjoyed trivia games. I had recently purchased the "Catholic Trivia" game. Every day I would put a few question cards in my jacket pocket, and I would spend my lunch break quizzing my new friend. I found that this normal activity often provided the level of comfort she needed before talking about more serious issues.

One day she told me that when the hospital chaplain visited her the previous evening, she told him that she was ready to die, but she could not understand why the Lord would not take her. "He told me that maybe the Lord was giving me the time I needed to take care of some unfinished business." "Well, he is the chaplain, and I am just a seminarian in training," I said in reply. "It is certainly true that we do not always understand God's ways." "I will certainly give that some thought," she said as she drifted off to sleep.

The next day I went in for our lunchtime visit. Two of her friends were visiting. I told her that I would come back later, but she told me to come in and join the party. Her friends were sitting in the chairs that were on the side of the bed closest to the door. I squeezed in so I could sit in the chair that was on the other side of the bed, closest to the wall and the window. The four of us played an enjoyable round of "Catholic Trivia" before her friends left.

A few minutes later, the woman's husband entered. He immediately walked over to the bed to give his wife a kiss. As he leaned towards her, but before I had a chance to excuse myself, the woman said to her husband, "Darling, I think that the reason the Lord is not ready to take me yet is because he wants to give me time to confess something to you." I wanted to scream out and say, "Wait, don't say another word until I leave," but I don't think she even realized I was still in the room. She continued confessing to her husband, saying, "Many years ago when we were having troubles in our marriage, I made a terrible mistake and I cheated on you."

I wanted to crawl under the bed or jump out the window, but all I could do at this point was hold my breath, hoping that somehow I would become invisible.

Without a moment of hesitation, the man looked at his wife and said, "I love you." Then he sat down on the edge of the bed, carefully lifted her into his arms, and held her as gently as he could. He kept repeating the words, "I love you, I love you, I love you." I knew this was the moment when I could make my escape. I quickly got up from the chair and quietly tiptoed out of the room, giving the couple the privacy they deserved.

Whenever I remember that sacred moment, I think of the line from the song that is sung as Jean Valjean is dying in the musical production of Victor Hugo's novel, *"Les Miserables"*, *"To love another person is to see the face of God."* I know that I saw the face of God that day. That kind gentleman loved his wife the way God loves us. It is the way Pope Francis is inviting all God's children in this world to love one another during the Jubilee Year. "It is hardly an exaggeration to say that this is a 'visceral' love," the Holy Father says when he describes this kind of love. "It gushes forth from the depths naturally, full of tenderness and compassion, indulgence and mercy."

That day I witnessed a sacramental celebration, an outward sign of the presence of God, and it brought Luke's beloved parable to life for me. And every day since, whenever I remember how that gentleman held his wife in his arms, I know that he was the living embodiment of the love and mercy of the Father, the fullest expression of the law of love. This love of God the Father was made incarnate in Jesus, the Son. As his disciples, we are called to do the same.

We are truly blessed. In our faith tradition we are able to ritualize the power of God's mercy and pardon through the sacraments of healing and reconciliation. The Sacrament of Reconciliation is a time when we can sit down with the church's minister who represents Christ and discuss the most serious ways in which we have wandered away from our loving God and Father. As we listen to the words of absolution, we resolve, with the help of God's grace, to perform an act of penance as a way of showing that we want to amend our lives.

In the early years of my priesthood, I would simply ask people to say a few prayers as a penance. Now I ask them to also consider performing an act of kindness or charity to show God that they are truly sorry for their sins and begin to make the necessary changes in their lives that will put them back on the path towards holiness. I find that this form of penance helps raise the person's conscious awareness of the ongoing process of reconciliation and conversion.

The Sacrament of the Eucharist is by its very nature a sacrament of reconciliation. Each time we gather to give the Lord praise and offer the great prayer of thanksgiving, we begin by calling to mind our sins, and we ask God for mercy and forgiveness. I encourage people to pay attention to the words of all the prayers offered by the priest throughout the celebration, prayers that are offered in the name of *all* who gather in *common union* (hence, communion).  Time and time again during the celebration of the Eucharist, we ask for God's mercy.

The holy season of Lent is the sacramental time when we reflect upon our lives and consider how we may have lost our way.  Lent can be described as a "homecoming of the soul."  We return to the place where we will be at home – in the loving embrace of the Father.  Luke's beloved parable touches the hearts of so many people because it reminds us that if we are honest with ourselves, we can see how we have behaved like one of the sons.  By fasting and doing good works, and through prayer and reflection, we find our way back to the One who has been grieving ever since we lost our way, the Loving Parent who has been waiting and watching for our return.

During the Holy Year of Mercy, Pope Francis is inviting us to rediscover the loving nature of the Father of Mercy.  He is in no way diminishing the fact that one day we will stand in judgment before God, but he wants the Church to share the *good news* that God's justice is *always* tempered by mercy.

I believe that the Church has been blessed with a special gift in the person of Pope Francis.  Now more than ever, the world needs his message of healing and hope.  If human beings are ever to develop the capacity to love one another the way God loves us, to accept our differences, and learn to forgive one another, we must begin by rediscovering the Divinity whose very nature is love.  Jesus is the great Mediator, the only begotten Son, who shows us what it means to be fully human.  The spark of the Divine that is within us can enkindle a fire of love that will shine forth in the way we treat one another.  When that happens, we rise to the fullness of our humanity.  This is what we pray for when we receive the Body and Blood of Christ in the Eucharist.  St. Augustine often said, "Become what you receive," when he offered the bread and wine to his people.

When Jesus said, "This is my Body," he was describing the embodiment of compassion and forgiveness that resided in his heart and soul.  This is the Bread of Life we receive in the Eucharist.  And the Cup of Salvation we receive is the love and mercy that flowed through his veins and was poured out in the blood he shed on the cross.  The cross is a powerful symbol.  It becomes the bridge that carries us from death to new life.  The outstretched arms of our Lord on the cross are a reminder to us that he is calling out to all who may have lost their way.

"Softly and tenderly Jesus is calling.
Calling to you and to me.
Though we have sinned He has mercy and pardon,
Pardon for you and for me.
Come home, come home,
You who are sinners come home.
Earnestly, desperately, Jesus is calling,
Calling O sinner come home"

*"Softly and Tenderly Jesus is Calling"*
**Will L. Thompson, pub. 1880**
**Copyright:  Public Domain**

# About the Author

Father Len Fecko has been a priest of the Archdiocese of Cincinnati for twenty-six years. He has been in parish ministry and has served as a campus minister at the University of Cincinnati and Miami University of Ohio. He received a BA in Psychology and an MS in Counseling from Miami. He completed a year of specialized studies in Gerontology at Miami University and the University of Hawaii. He received his Master of Divinity from the Athenaeum of Ohio and was ordained in 1989. He received an MA in Pastoral Studies from Seattle University in 1995.

Fr. Len has been an adjunct professor in the Gerontology program at Mt. St. Joseph University in Cincinnati and in the School of Theology and Ministry at Seattle University.

In 2005, Fr. Len suffered a massive stroke which forced him to resign from full-time ministry. In 2011 he was asked to give a retreat for the Sisters of Notre Dame of Namur in Cincinnati. Since that time he has given retreats to religious communities and parish groups. He says proudly, "Now I can say that I have "soul sisters" all over the United States!"

This reflection on "the parable of the prodigal" began as a homily several years ago. His homily became the catalyst for a longer reflection which he has given in parishes during the season of Lent.

Sept. 11, 2015, marked ten years since he had his stroke. "I wanted to prove to myself that I still had the capacity to accomplish something that demonstrates that my brain is still functioning. When I read the reference Pope Francis made to the parable of the lost son, I knew the perfect time had come for me to put my reflections on paper. It is my intent that when people read my reflections, they will come to know the God of love and compassion who has been present to me in every chapter of my life."

---

**To contact Father Len Fecko regarding his "Aging Gracefully, Becoming Fully Graced" retreat for your parish or religious community, to inquire about future publications, or to discuss plans for a parish mission, send an email to: lfecko@icloud.com or call (513) 699-5326.**